DESERTS!

A MY INCREDIBLE WORLD PICTURE BOOK

MY INCREDIBLE WORLD

Deserts are barren, dry land regions characterized by low rainfall, sparse vegetation, and extreme temperatures.

About one-fifth of the land on Earth is made up of deserts.

They form as a result of specific atmospheric pressure, geographic location, and the planet's rotation.

Deserts aren't always hot and sandy. Sometimes they can be very cold and snow-covered — like the South Pole.

There are 23 deserts on Earth, the largest 3 being the Antarctic Desert, Arctic Desert, and Sahara Desert.

There are 5 major desert types: **Subtropical**, **Coastal**, **Rain Shadow**, **Interior**, and **Polar**.

Subtropical deserts are characterized by hot, dry conditions and low rainfall.

Coastal deserts are near seas and oceans, with cooler temperatures and occasional fog or mist.

Rain shadow deserts form near mountain ranges, which block moist air and precipitation.

Interior deserts are located far from coastlines and are typically surrounded by land.

Polar deserts are in polar regions that have very low temperatures and limited precipitation.

Some animals, such as camels, scorpions, rattlesnakes, and meerkats, have adapted to live in deserts.

Various plants have also evolved to thrive in these conditions, including cacti, succulents and some shrubs!

Deserts are among the hottest places on Earth, with daytime temperatures soaring well above 100°F (38°C).

At night, however, temperatures
in some deserts can plummet
close to or below freezing!

Rainfall in the desert is infrequent and low, averaging less than 10 inches (25 cm) per year.

Snowfall in non-polar deserts is also rare, with very light accumulations that often melt quickly.

Many deserts have **sand dunes**, which are mounds or ridges of sand formed by the wind.

A desert **oasis** is a lush area where water is found, providing a vital resource for plants and animals.

A **mirage** is an optical illusion of distant objects or water, caused by light bending due to air temperature.

Desert ecosystems are delicate and easily disrupted by human activities, so it's important to protect them.

Deserts are incredible!

Made in United States
Troutdale, OR
04/03/2025

30310222R00017